A Brief Guide to
Selling Your Business

With Minimum Stress
at Maximum Price

A Process Overview for
Business Owners

by

Richard Mowrey

Valuation and
Ownership Transfer
Expert

Get Answers to 7 Important Questions

FREE! A LIST OF WHAT SERIOUS BUYERS WILL ASK EVERY SELLER
www.RichMowrey.com/Buyers

This book was written and published for your personal use and enjoyment based on the knowledge and experience of the author. It is sold subject to the condition that it will not be circulated in any form, including photocopying or recording.

The author makes no representations or warranties with respect to the accuracy or completeness of the contents in this book. This work is a process overview only. No warranty may be created by use of any part of the information provided. Please be advised that the matters discussed herein are not accounting, tax, legal, or explicit transaction advice. All such information is provided for general understanding only. No statements as to the current regulation, accounting, tax, or legal statutes made herein should be relied on for specific business decisions. The advice and strategies may not be suitable for application in every transaction. Readers should independently verify all information through their own investigations. Every business owner should follow the advice of their own personal transaction, valuation, legal, accounting, tax, and financial advisors. These knowledgeable professionals should be the source of precise, timely advice for individual situations.

Published by: Groundhog New Media

ISBN: 978-0-9978801-7-5

Version 2021.03.15

Book design by Amit Dey

Table of Contents

"Time is more valuable than money.
You can get more money, but you cannot
get more time!"

Introduction

The sale of a business is probably the most important transaction in the life of a business owner ... for many reasons. This process overview is provided to give business owners an early appreciation of what to expect as they approach the sale of their company.

The book should be used to add a basic understanding of what to expect in a business sale. It poses and answers the seven key questions that business owners have as they consciously move toward the biggest deal of their careers. As noted, this is a summary of key areas where your personal knowledge will make a difference as you proceed. Additional resources the reader can turn to for a deeper understanding of the "business sale process" are provided within the text ... or in the appendix.

Many business owners defer thinking about and preparing for the sale of their business. The fact that you are now starting should put you ahead of the pack. Early, effective preparation for your "someday sale" will pay significant dividends and smooth out some of the "bumps" along the way. The process overview will get you started on your personal education in this important area of business ownership, so you can be better equipped to reach your financial and personal goals.

"Sometimes if you want to see a change for the better, you have to take things into your own hands."

– *Clint Eastwood*

A Brief Guide to Selling Your Business With Minimum Stress at Maximum Price

It is your business. It is far from just a job. You've put years of work, worry, and money into its growth. But at some point—no matter how much you are a part of your business—you will ask this question:

"When and How Should I Sell My Business?"

There may be good reasons why these thoughts have arrived. Maybe you are becoming more aware that you are moving close to retirement. Maybe you see the future requiring addtional capital. Or maybe you are just ready for some new challenges.

As you consciously address the coming ownership transition, you will find yourself posing these seven questions:

- **"When should I sell my business?"**
- **"Will the sale proceeds fully fund my dream retirement?"**
- **"How do I locate a qualified buyer?"**
- **"After I find a buyer, what problems will I face?"**
- **"How do I set a price for my company?"**
- **"Who should handle the deal negotiations?"**
- **"Am I really ready to step away from my business?"**

For the first-time seller or even the experienced seller, selling your business is a process that uniquely combines both unknown pitfalls and significant opportunities. Aside from achieving a fair price with favorable tax treatment, you would like to put your life's work into the right hands.

This brief guide was written to help you find the answers to the questions you may have about selling a business. It is by no means intended to try to convince you to sell now or in the future. It is designed to give you a picture of the process and to encourage you to begin preparing today for your "someday sale."

The information is here to provide you with a few guidelines about how to go about it once you have made the decision to market your business. We will also suggest some considerations that are required to make the most informed decisions possible.

This brief review is not meant to be a complete guide to a preparation and execution process that has literally hundreds of important steps. If you would like to go deeper and gather additional information about the best practices in "value enhancement" and "preparation of your business for a sale," please refer to these books:

- **When Is the Right Time to Sell My Business?**

- **How Can I Increase the Value of My Business?**

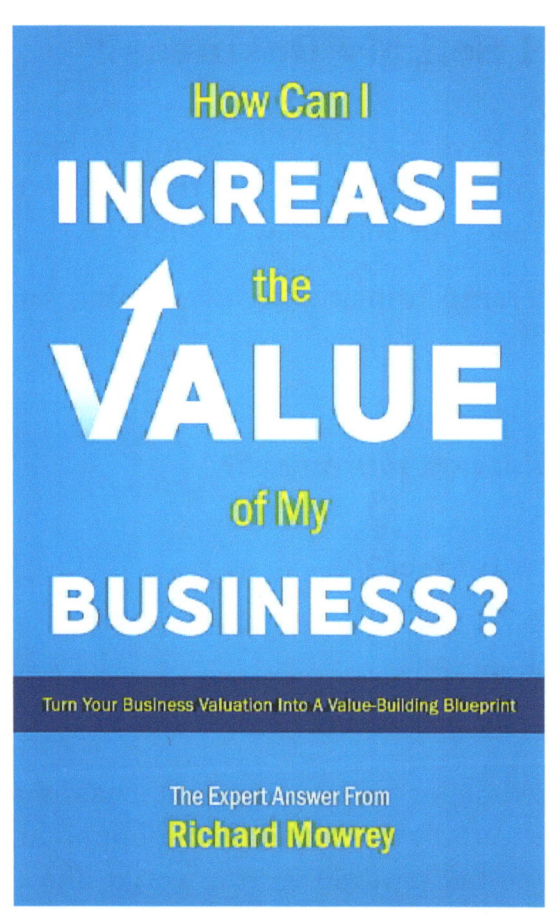 

These two books will take you quickly and quietly along your journey so you can cut the ties to your business without regrets.

Q1: When should I sell my business?

A1: The answer to the question is easy. But it creates related questions with more complexity. There are two primary parts to this answer. The first is from your personal viewpoint:

Sell Your Business
When You Are Ready to Sell!

People sell their businesses for any number of reasons.

Typically, here are some more personal reasons:

- To start a brand new business possibly in a new location
- To deal with personal or family health problems
- To address burnout and a decline in the interest in the business
- To find a solution for being unable to transfer the business to the next generation
- To recognize that the next business development phase requires new and broader management skills and added capital

Retirement fits into this list too, but if you are considering retiring, start planning well ahead. In fact, when selling for any reason, if possible, you should begin to restructure the company to reduce your operating risk, improve profitability, and start to identify potential types of buyers years ahead of your target date for the sale. Early, effective preparation for the sale will provide measurable benefits. This preparation should involve you, the owner, as well as the business. It is much harder to step away from your life's work than you might think it would be. Positioning yourself for this change is important to the business and to you.

It is also entirely possible that an optimal buyer might appear unannounced. If you have prepared yourself, you will be in a much better position to consider their offer and act on it. So, getting ready early can be especially important for several reasons.

The second part of the answer to the question of "When to sell?" comes from a value maximizing viewpoint. You want to sell not only when you are personally ready but:

Sell Your Business
When Your Business Is Ready to Sell!

It is easier to sell a business when it is doing well, improving regularly, and shaping up well financially. That is how and when you will get the best price and terms.

Always remember:

"Buyers invest in the future of a business but "largely" base their decision to buy on past performance."

Many factors can influence the timing of a sale, including the condition of the economy, current business trends *(what's "hot" ... in demand in the market)*, interest rates, etc. You also may want to adjust the sale date to allow for the rollout of a new product that will have an impact over the next few years. The market conditions are really a separate consideration. The first order of business is preparing the business operation.

This involves

- Good strategic and business planning and execution
- Increases in gross and net margins *(to add cash flow)*
- Development of a sustainable revenue growth pattern
- Adding repeatable systems to ensure consistent results
- Building out of the management team to gain needed strength

The key is to assess the current position of the business and understand what future value goal must be realized before the transfer is planned. This preparation should bring the business closer and closer to being ready for a sale. There is great value in each and every step in this direction. The "readier" your business is, the easier it will be for you to say "yes" to an early offer from a highly qualified buyer.

The measuring and management of business value can make a monumental difference. Simple steps to improve the "rewards" of ownership and to reduce the "risk" of operating any business can, at times, double or triple the business's value.

The broader market must be separately considered. Your business is likely to be performing better if your industry is doing well within a generally good economy. To the extent that you can time your decision beyond "When the Business is Ready!" it is advantageous to sell when your industry is growing and "in demand" by the "investor groups" or "individuals" who see the benefits of industry ownership.

"Part of success is preparation on purpose."

"Do not let the fear of striking out...hold you back."

— *Babe Ruth*

Q2: Will the sale proceeds fully fund my dream retirement?

A2: You will only know the answer to the question of "how much is enough" … by formally assessing the gap, if any, your business sale must fill. Most business owners have the vast majority of their wealth tied up in their business. You can make estimates of the "net investable cash" your business may bring someday. You can guess about how much you will need to live the lifestyle of your dreams. Unfortunately, these estimates and guesses may be off the mark.

You do not want to be close to your planned retirement date and find out your business is worth far less than you think it should be. Nor do you want to learn too late that life in retirement can, in the early years, be significantly more expensive than you believed … especially if you are traveling and maintaining multiple residences.

The best way to determine "where you are" and "where you need to be"—from a projected business value perspective—is to have your business professionally valued by an knowledgeable expert.

In concert with the report development, you want to find (if you don't already have one) an experienced financial planner who has a top reputation. The financial planner can assemble and analyze your current and projected assets … net of your business. And then provide you with the information you need, which is the amount of "earning assets" you will want to have in place to generate the future annual income to match your planned future expenses.

Once you have that "target asset amount" in your sights, you will know what gap your business must fill when it is sold. That number and the value estimate from the business valuator might match. You may already be in a great position ... or you may need to take steps to increase the value of your business to reach the new goal you now have crystallized.

The business valuator, if you find the right one, should become a trusted advisor for you going forward. He or she can help you focus on the changes that will begin to consistently increase the value of your business.

The operative and valuable quote is:

"What gets measured ... gets done!"

By monitoring and managing the value going forward from this point, you should find positive progress with welcome results. This value-measurement process will give you the answer to the question about whether the sale of your business will fund your retirement as you are planning. This is your real-time answer.

Q3: How do I locate a qualified buyer?

A3: As with any marketing problem, the first step is to analyze the situation and identify the best potential buyers. A key employee, a supplier, or a competitor might have an interest in acquiring your business. These potential buyers may or may not be your best options. And ... you need to plan when and how you engage any of them.

Consider all your own contacts and networks.

Most potential buyers fall into three categories:

1. Individuals, for the most part, buy businesses with a purchase price of under $3 million and/or profits of less than $500,000 annually.

2. Businesses marginally above this size generally require a down payment *(equity portion of corporate capital)* which is out of reach for many individuals. Consequently, the buying prospects become local investment partnerships or smaller regional corporations seeking growth.

3. Larger private and public corporations and investment groups make up the third category. They seek out companies with a purchase price up to $30 million. Corporate buyers (private and public) and investment companies (private equity groups) usually look for a business with at least $20 million in sales volume and/or $4 million in pre-tax profits annually. At times, they will consider additions to an existing investment in their portfolio. *(These "add-ons" can be of any size ... but typically they require earnings greater than $1 million.)*

Owners may start by offering the business to a key employee (or management group). This is often a major mistake. Certainly, if this person or persons share the future vision for the company and have the financial strength to complete a sale, that can work. But too often this is not the case and the situation creates several new problems.

First, your employee or management group may not have the risk tolerance to be business owners. You do it naturally. Others may not. Also, if the prospective new owner does not have the financial strength to complete a sale on commercial banking terms, they will look to you to finance the deal. This can create a difficult discussion that should be avoided unless there is a good reason for you to go down this path.

Next, suppliers or competitors may or may not be good buyers. The relationship may change once you start an investigation process with them if the deal does not go through. Certainly, any communications with competitors requires great care. These information releases should be taken only after you have taken steps to protect proprietary processes and key vendor or customer lists. Consequently, these two groups of prospective buyers should be staged later in the marketing process and addressed with due caution.

Business owners are often tempted to locate and contact buyers personally. *(Those already discussed and other types of buyers.)* Doing this through advertising, referrals, and the industry's "grapevine" has its risks and may not bubble up the best buyers either. Not only is such an "owner's search" difficult, but it is also a time-consuming task and may not leave you—the seller—in the best negotiating position. It can also compromise the confidentiality of the sale.

A better choice would be to use an experienced intermediary to contact and interface with potential buyers. *(This is something we will explore more extensively later in this guide.)* A professional intermediary will provide the critical experience and knowledge necessary in mergers and acquisitions. By providing access to a diverse network of potential buyers, an experienced professional can help you fully develop the market opportunities for your business.

This approach also permits the business owner to focus on their primary "day job" … running the business to get optimal financial results.

Please remember: Buyers "assess the past" and "buy the future."

The better the business is operating, the easier it will be to sell and to negotiate a superior price and terms. Experienced dealmakers will keep you informed every step of the way so you can make all the key decisions. You never relinquish your position as the business owner and should insist on reviewing all marketing plans, including the specific buyers who will be "confidentially contacted" at the beginning of the marketing process. Experienced transaction advisors are very good at maintaining confidentiality in each step of a deal, and in the extensive negotiations that take place throughout the entire preparation and sale process.

Please remember that your buyer search should be based on your specific objectives for the ultimate transaction results. If you want to have a high probability that the entire workforce will be maintained, you may not want to seek "strategic buyers." These are buyers who are primarily interested in the technical versus the financial attributes of your business. Ask your dealmaker about buyers who might fall into this category.

"If you want to be truly happy, set a goal that commands your thoughts, liberates your energy, and inspires you with hope."

— Andrew Carnegie

Q4: After I find a buyer, what problems will I face?

A4: Each sale is unique but there are key problem areas common to most transactions. For simplicity's sake, we'll touch on only five here.

1. Negotiations

If there is one word that sums up what happens in a business sale, it's detailed negotiation. It is absolutely essential that your primary negotiator should have at least the same level of sophistication as the buyer and his support staff.

The vast majority of lower middle market business buyers today are professionals who spend all of their time identifying and acquiring privately held businesses.

Very few sellers have the negotiating skills or up-to-date information about transaction strategies, terms, and other considerations. Even if they do, they are often too close and too emotionally involved in the sale to be as effective as a third-party professional.

You might arrange to use your attorney or Certified Public Accountant (CPA) as your primary business negotiator. Although skilled in

their respective fields *(where they definitely should be involved)*, they are often less knowledgeable about the business aspects of a sale. They normally do not have extensive buyer networks or past experience with different types of professional buyers. They also can be limited by professional restrictions and their relationship to the various parties in the deal. This is where an experienced third-party intermediary or business broker can make a tremendous contribution.

2. Legal Consideration

A great deal of legal scrutiny is required in any company sale. For example, the transaction may involve a sale of stock or assets. Service agreements such as a noncompete and consulting may be part of the purchase, as well. Purchase agreements with warrants, indemnifications, terms, and conditions must be negotiated and structured.

Always select a legal firm experienced in the sale of businesses to provide this critically important legal counsel, to prepare these legal documents, and to support your decisions. An experienced attorney with a very focused practice in mergers and acquisitions can often be significantly more efficient. It is not the hourly fee that matters ... it is the productivity and the final work product that counts most. These are areas where knowledge and experience can result in a much better-balanced deal for you.

3. Taxes

As an owner, your true results from the sale are directly dependent on the percentage of the sale price paid out in taxes. It is vital that your CPA, attorney, and intermediary work to minimize your tax burden. Proper structuring of a sale can have a tremendous effect on your net cash from the sale.

When you make your early assessment on the value of your business and your financial retirement goal, you should address transaction taxes. This element in every transaction is material to the results you will achieve and to the financial freedom you are seeking.

4. Personnel

This is an area where you want the best human resource advisors you can afford. You do not want to disrupt your valued work force. And you want to give consideration to all involved. The potential for changes, if any, in company and/or employee relations should be understood and discussed in detail before beginning a sale process.

For example: What happens to a union during a sale can depend on whether the sale is of stock or assets. It may also be affected by the terms of the union contract, how the employees feel about the union, and the needs or requirements of both buyer and seller. It's an important area of negotiations and must be handled carefully. As a general rule, whether union or nonunion, good employees can often benefit from a change in ownership.

5. Costs

Legal fees may run up to $25,000 on a $1 million transaction and may total $40,000 to $50,000 on a $4 to $5 million sale. These figures should not deter you from retaining the best legal help you can get. Talk to several firms to determine their experience and aptitude with these kinds of transactions.

CPAs' fees tend to fall in the $10,000 to $20,000 range for all but the larger transactions. (*If there is a lot of due diligence work, these fees could be proportionally higher.*)

Your current CPA firm should be able to organize and establish the credibility of your financial data and also work effectively with the buyer's CPA.

In today's digital environment, historic financial and other company information is normally loaded into a "cloud-holding system" so the information can be released in a timely manner. Early preparation for this delivery is a great benefit when you are trying to maintain the momentum needed in a deal.

Intermediary fees range from about 8% to10% on most smaller transactions and are typically 3% to 6% on a multi-million-dollar sale. For example: On an average $3 million sale, expect to pay professional fees of from $125,000 to $175,000.

A good intermediary earns these fees over and over again by getting the best price for the company and structuring the transaction to maximize the net cash proceeds you receive. And...maybe more importantly, these professionals can help you avoid a myriad of bothersome post-closing issues and problems.

Before hiring an intermediary, find out on what the professional fees will be based. And when they will be paid as the process develops. Most experienced, professional intermediaries require a retainer and monthly operating fees to cover initial and continuing marketing costs.

Be aware that the fees may be affected if real estate or leasing is involved in the transaction. There are different rules and regulations regarding sales of real estate in different states. Some states require a real estate license to assist the transfer and sale of real property. You should discuss this requirement, the related sales costs, and the actual process to be followed with your advisors.

Q5: How do I set a price for my company?

A5: We recommend that owners not try to establish a price themselves. Aside from being too close to the company, few business owners have the experience, information, or tools to determine their business's projected value in the marketplace.

You're better off calling in an outside, independent professional business valuator to value the business. In addition, your intermediary and/or other advisors should have sufficient experience in the business of selling companies like yours. Such current selling experience should help develop a price and strategy by adding some understanding of recent market trends.

In order to set the price, the first step will be to establish a Fair Market Value (FMV) for the business's tangible and intangible assets. This is done through a "recast" of the financial data to reflect the company's actual transferrable assets within a professional valuation. This may not be the price … but it certainly establishes the general "target range" for a transaction. This should be the amount on which you and your advisor agree you will sell, if it can be achieved. You should not begin a sale process if this value is not sufficient to fund your retirement or if you cannot accept it for some other reason.

The recast value differs from "book" value in that anything that would not be included in the sale of assets and liabilities is removed from the financial statement (i.e., personal vehicles, owner notes, etc.). What's left is adjusted to real market value—including inventory, accounts receivable, and equipment—thereby providing a more accurate assessment of the company's hard asset value.

This is the first part of a several-part analysis to determine the fair market value of the business.

For manufacturing companies, equipment appraisals may be required to structure financing. It is often advisable, therefore, to have a formal equipment appraisal completed before the business is put on the market. *(This appraisal should provide an estimate of "market-value-in-place.")*

Most experienced buyers will also determine the liquidation value of the business. This valuation reference point helps the buyer assess the downside risks and is information that the seller should also have during negotiations.

The other key part of the valuation process involves the development of a Recast Income Statement. When prepared for tax reporting, the income statement may include expenses that have only a limited relationship to the future operation of the business, such as an owner vehicle, retirement plan, entertainment, or life insurance. In the recast statement, these items are adjusted to show the total earning power of the business. This is the income available to the new owners for capital investments, increases in working capital, payment of taxes to determine the net after-tax income benefit of ownership. This figure is then used to analytically determine the company's value.

Buyers look at the adjusted income figures over a three-to-five-year period. The average or weighted-average income coupled with growth factors is then used to project the Buyer's Future Return On Investment. Presently, buyers are looking for a 20% to 30% after-tax return, although for a stable business with a promising future, they may consider an after-tax return of 15% to 20% in exchange for the reduced risk.

As stated before, buyers are buying the future, but they will base their purchase on the past performance of the company and its current prospects. The historic growth rate of the industry and the historic growth rate of the business are critical elements in any final determination of the expected return, since a buyer will only want to pay for a projection of the past trend. In preparing the business for sale—getting it ready—this fact should be completely understood. Therefore, it is extremely important that a seller document the basis for past trends and the reason for any changes in future expectations. It should be recognized that the buyer will want to discount future growth projections that are not clearly indicated by the recent past performance of the business. The price range acceptable to a qualified

buyer will be heavily affected by his/her level of confidence in the **future growth of the company's net cash flows**.

The desired return on investment adjusted for the impact of income growth, together with the Fair Market Value of the Net Assets, determines the price a qualified buyer will pay. In addition, the financing component of the capital in the transaction will directly impact the percentage of cash at closing. These outcomes will be limited by the seller's ability to communicate the underlying value of the business assets and the future earning capability of the business. Clearly, the recognition of these facts suggests that a consistent pattern of growth in revenue, gross margins, and net cash flow will help a seller achieve the highest possible selling price.

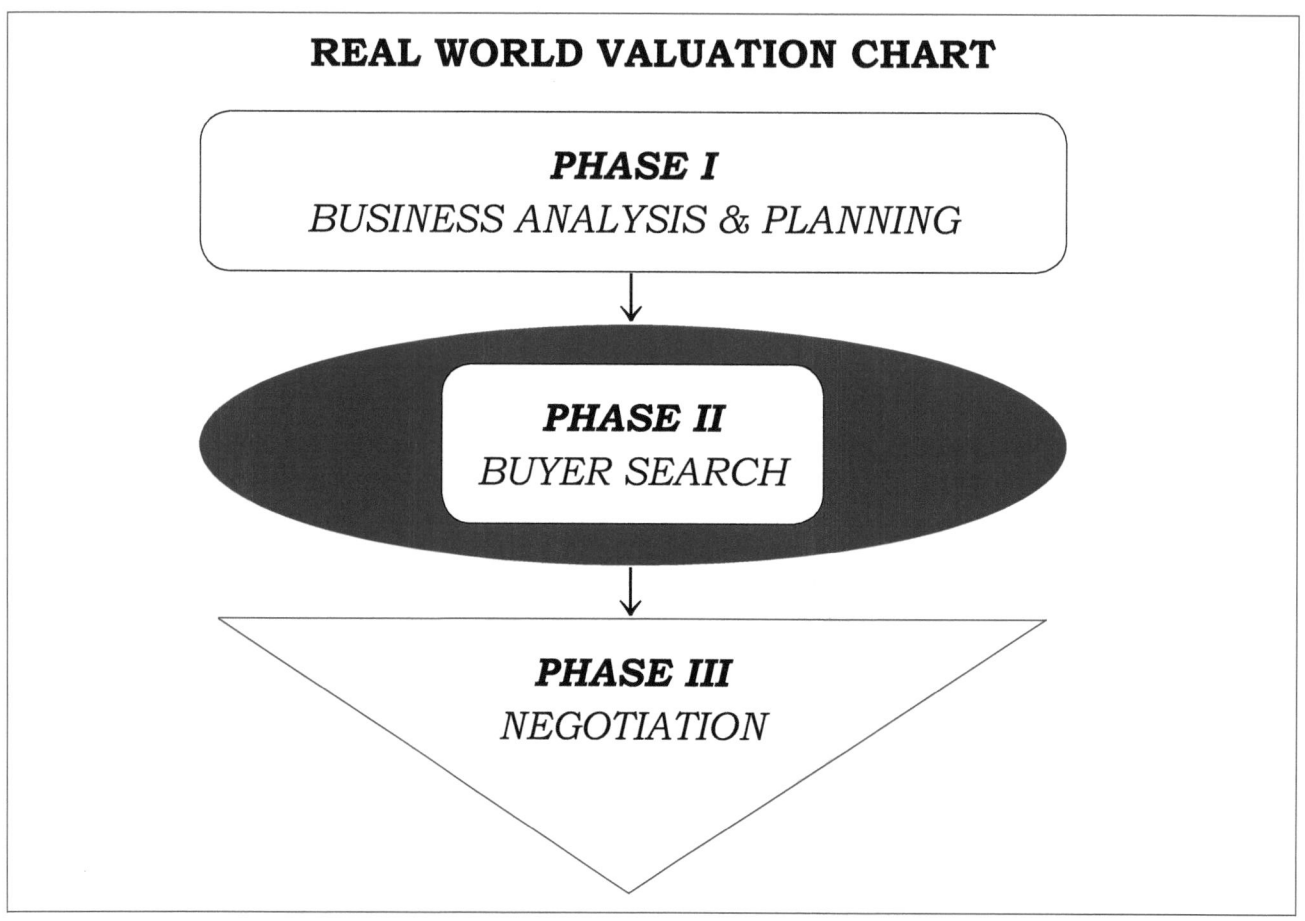

The chart above shows the controlling factors for the actual selling price of your business. **It is the "Market"!**

The better prepared you are, the better prepared the business is, and the better that the future prospects for the business are presented ... the more likely you are to optimize the potential price and terms!

With effective early planning and transaction process efforts, you should be able to achieve a price at or above your "target value" ... to provide for a retirement of your dreams.

What kind of payment should I expect?
Can I get all cash?

You might be able to get a cash payment, but you will probably have to discount the purchase price ... maybe by as much as 20%. When the owner's note is properly collateralized, you're usually money ahead to take 70% to 80% in payment at closing and a note for the balance. Here are the terms for a couple of sample transactions:

1. Buyer down payment (equity)   30%
   Bank financing   50%
   Owner carry note   20%

The owner note may be amortized over five years, or over as much as ten years. Normally, the slower amortization over seven or ten years has a balloon payment at the end of five years. Interest might be set at prime rate plus 1% or 2%. Payments of principal and interest for "seller notes" are typically monthly or quarterly. The note to be carried by the owner should be secured by a second position on the assets of the company and the personal guarantee of the buyer.

Larger transactions would rarely have as much as 20% in a seller note. If the price gap is over 10% to 15%, other elements might be negotiated into the deal before reaching for a larger portion of the selling price in "seller financing." Professional buyers typically will be putting more equity into a deal. Usually, 35% to 40%. An example deal structure could take this form:

2. Buyer "equity"   40%
   Commercial funding   50% (Bank lending)
   Seller financing   10% (No buyer guarantees)

In down markets, private equity groups may increase their equity contribution to as much as 50%. These professional dealmakers often make use of alternative financing methods. They also can provide a recapitalization option for the owner. This approach permits retention of a non-controlling interest in the company going forward. These types of "sales" should be analyzed before you begin the process to establish that such a result is an acceptable objective.

3. Buyer down payment   20%
   Owner carry note   80%

This could be the type of structure worked out for an "internal management purchase." Owner note might be amortized over ten years with a balloon payment at the end of five or seven years. Interest normally will be at a fixed rate of

2% to 3% above prime. In some cases, there are interest-only payments for the first two years, then principal and interest are paid quarterly until the balloon payment date.

You might be asking, "Why would I want to carry such a large portion of the total transaction?" You would make this decision for two reasons. First, the bank lending available to the "management team" might be limited to only 40% to 50% of the deal. In such a case, you would be behind the bank on all the collateral and be carrying almost as much of a debt level. That would make it prudent to be in first position for repayment by taking the entire financial package.

Second, you should only be willing to put yourself into this position if you really want the current manager(s) to become the new owner(s) and you have confidence in their abilities to manage the business and pay you within the planned terms (i.e., you are taking the risk to create a certain outcome). This picture is why it was mentioned early that you should carefully consider if and when to offer the business to the management team. As noted, they may not be interested and they may not have the required personal assets to use for the "down payment" *(owners' equity)*.

Balancing: Terms and Security

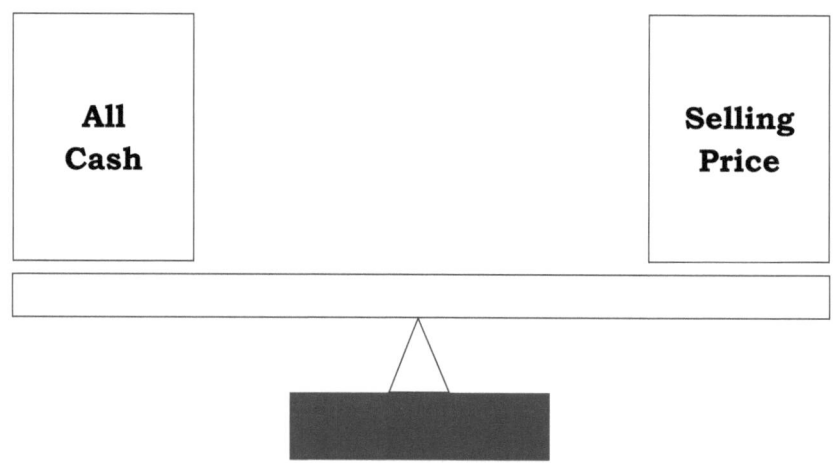

Please note: When you first complete your valuation, work with your advisors to determine the impact of taxes on your net proceeds from the sale.

In addition, this early "picture" of your "after-tax" results will be of significant value in the preparation for price negotiations and your understanding of the potential need for ... and magnitude of "seller financing"... to close the transaction.

Q6: Who should handle the deal negotiations?

A6. Find and hire a professional business broker or intermediary to handle all phases ... especially the negotiation phase. Here are the questions that answer generates:

Why is this a good option?

Who should I use?

How do I choose that person or firm?

We have already mentioned a couple of other possibilities, such as your CPA and your attorney. We could also add *general business consultants* to that list.

But, as we said before, while they are all excellent resources to draw upon within their own areas of expertise, very few of these professionals have the combination of market knowledge, transaction experience, or negotiating skills of a professional intermediary.

A professional business intermediary can oversee the entire sale, from initial valuation through marketing, to final closing—all with an eye for opportunities based on current market trends.

You should look for a business intermediary who is totally familiar with business sales in general and with the type of business you are selling.

Choose your intermediary like you would choose a pilot. Do not let a crop duster fly your airliner. Find an intermediary with a proven history of dealing with your size of business.

There are two different groups of focused and experienced business sale advisors:

General Business Brokers: These professionals normally handle businesses with selling prices up to $3 million. Most of their transactions will have selling prices under $1 million. They will have extensive databases and knowledge of individual buyers.

Middle-Market Intermediaries: These key professional advisors work with businesses that have selling prices between $3 million and $30 million. *(And at times even larger deals.)* They treat each engagement with a seller as a major project that might take twelve to eighteen months … or longer. If you can find and begin working with a good middle market advisor early in your preparation process, that is absolutely the best approach. They can add immeasurable insight into "what sells" and "what you need to do to get your business ready to sell."

A good business broker or intermediary should be adept at confirming business value ranges based on previous sales and current market conditions. He or she should also be able to give you a realistic time frame for the sale.

Experience is vital, but the ability of the intermediary to understand the primary concerns for your business and your family are more important. Hire the intermediary with the same care that you would take with any key professional. Do it as early as possible.

The right intermediary will be able to manage the transaction for you, or, if you prefer, simply to provide needed "a la cart" support in some or all of the phases of the transaction. In a complex situation, it is critical to be able to discuss problems and concerns with a knowledgeable advisor.

There are members of different professional organizations who can help you. *(There is a list of some of these in Appendix B.)* Do not only look at the depth of individual experience but determine the advantages each different potential advisor may have as part of the various independent networks of general business brokers or mid-market professionals.

The preparation matters. The marketing matters. And … the deal negotiation and closing process matters. All of the nearly two hundred steps in this process requires execution in the proper sequence to achieve an optimal result.

Too many "good deals" are never closed because there was insufficient preparation of the business ... and/or the owner.

Yes ... the owner!

The sale of your business is an emotional process that you must prepare for. Otherwise, what should be small deal elements can "look" too large to you at exactly the wrong time. Let your advisor do the hard work and spend the necessary time with you to be sure you are really ready before you take your business to market. And ... let him/her keep you at a "safe distance" from the more difficult aspects of negotiations so you can make the required decisions with a clear, sound look at the impact of the decision at hand!

Before retaining any business broker or intermediary, a seller should find out this information:

- Their background—what kind of work they've been doing.
- How long they have been serving your size and type of business.
- The relative success of their efforts.
- Whether they understand your business in detail, not just on the surface.
- Whether they are familiar with the tax and legal considerations of your sale.
- How and where they will advertise your business.
- What kind of industry and support contacts they have.
- Whether they have any national or international affiliations that might give your sale broader exposure.
- If they already have a buyer inventory appropriate for your business.

One important function of an intermediary is preserving the confidentiality of the sale. Although you do not want your sale to be so secret you limit your exposure, the proper level of confidentiality can help enhance your negotiating position and protect your ongoing company operations.

An intermediary can contact prospective buyers within your industry *(or even within your company)* to qualify them for interest and financial position, without revealing details of your identity. *A good intermediary will always require a non-disclosure agreement before releasing more than basic information to any potential buyer.*

Please remember: the dates in your scheduling planner are closer than you think! Now ... really *is* the time to assemble a professional advisory team to assist you in the biggest deal of your business career.

Intermediaries *(business brokers)* associated with professional networks have reputations for dedication and excellence. These professionals have the critical experience and the international support system to guide you through the sale process in a timely manner as shown in the three outlines below.

Phase I

- Development of a Confidential Seller's Profile
- Development of the Business Information Document
- Distribution of a Confidential Seller's Profile
- Buyer's Completion of a Confidentiality Agreement
- Distribution of the Business Information Document
- Establishment of a Buyer's Ability to Purchase Business

Phase II

- Facilities Inspection and Financial Analysis by Buyer(s)
- Preliminary Price and Terms Negotiations
- Deal Structuring *(Outline of an Agreement in Principle)*

Phase III

- Due Diligence Management to Completion
- Development of the Definitive Purchase Agreement
- Closing and Post-Closing Processes

"Formal education will make you a living. Self-education will make you a fortune!"

Q7: Am I really ready to step away from my business?

A7. Making the final decision to sell will be difficult without preparation and full consideration of all your alternatives. To complete a sale takes some perseverance. So, you must be ready and have the right team around you. If you have prepared your business and done the major things to prepare yourself, do not doubt the process. Make the decision. It can be freeing.

That said, you need to remember that there are over two hundred detailed steps in this sale process. Each one will need to be executed carefully to achieve the optimal result! You want to remain in the position of "team owner" and have your key advisors calling the plays on the field.

The vast majority of the negotiation within a "middle market transaction" or a larger "main street deal" takes place during the development of the Purchase and Sale Agreement. If this is your first or only business sale, it is important to be aware that the price and terms in the outline may change. *(That is, the price may go down and/ or some of the key terms may be questioned and removed or adjusted as a result of the due diligence process or negotiation tradeoffs. This is the reason for good, solid efforts on documentation of your business's operations and due diligence preparation. This is important.)* You and your advisor should discuss the nature of the activity so you can effectively prepare for the difficulties that may arrive during this period of time.

Ultimately, all of these ups and downs will even out if you are prepared and patient with yourself and your advisory team. A business sale can be very emotional, which is why it is important for you to be ready for this transition ... and to engage experienced counsel. Once the deal is successfully completed, you can relax and look forward to the new activities you have been planning and know that your business is in good hands for the future.

As you approach the transition point, you should be looking forward toward your financial freedom and to making good use of your time and liquid assets for yourself, your family, and your community!

APPENDIX

APPENDIX A – YOUR EXPERT ADVISORY TEAM

APPENDIX B – PROFESSIONAL ORGANIZATIONS

APPENDIX C – INFORMATION REQUIRED TO BEGIN A BUSINESS VALUATION

APPENDIX D – THE REAL ESTATE QUESTION

APPENDIX E – VALUE-ENHANCING BOOKS TO READ

APPENDIX A

YOUR EXPERT ADVISORY TEAM

- **Attorney**

- **Certified Public Accountant (CPA)**

- **Business Valuator**

- **Financial Planner**

- **Strategic and Business Planner**

- **Insurance Agent**

- **Intermediary or Business Broker**

- **Spouse**

Assembling a great group of personal advisors can make all the difference in a business sale process. Each of the advisors listed above will have a particular functional area of expertise to share and use for your benefit. Please take the time to find people who understand you and your business and are a good personal match for you. You will be glad you put the right people on your team!

APPENDIX B

PROFESSIONAL ORGANIZATIONS

International Business Brokers Association

The International Business Brokers Association (IBBA) is the world's largest professional community of business ownership transfer specialists. IBBA members primarily help owners complete "main street" business transactions.

M&A Source

M&A Source is a community of dealmakers, providing education and transaction opportunities for professionals. (*M&A* refers to mergers and acquisitions.) These acquisition and strategic advisors are dedicated to the support of transactions in the lower, middle market.

Alliance of Merger & Acquisition Advisors

The Alliance of Merger & Acquisition Advisors (AM&AA) is a membership organization that provides education, networking, and resources for a variety of professionals who do domestic, international, and cross-border merger-and-acquisition support for business owners.

American Society of Appraisers

The American Society of Appraisers (ASA) is a world renowned and respected international organization devoted to the appraisal profession. ASA is the oldest and only major appraisal organization designating members in all appraisal specialties.

National Association of Certified Valuators and Analysts

The National Association of Certified Valuators and Analysts supports the users of business valuation and financial litigation services—including damages determinations of all kinds—by training and certifying financial professionals in these disciplines. *(The Institute of Business Appraisers is now a part of this organization.)*

Accredited in Business Valuation

The Accredited in Business Valuation credential is granted exclusively by the AICPA to CPAs and qualified valuation professionals who demonstrate considerable expertise in valuation through their knowledge, skill, experience, and adherence to professional standards.

International Society of Business Appraisers

This organization is the newest professional group on the block. It focuses on valuation education and membership support toward smaller (main street) businesses and related appraisal assignments.

Canadian Institute of Chartered Business Valuators

The members of this organization are internationally recognized professionals known for having the judgement and analytical training necessary for a wide range of valuation-based needs. These projects include value measurement, value creation, and value protection.

APPENDIX C

INFORMATION REQUIRED
TO BEGIN A BUSINESS VALUATION

Additional information may be requested to complete the required full analysis to be performed by the valuation analyst.

1. <u>Financial Statements for the last five fiscal (or calendar) years</u> and <u>tax returns for the same five-year period</u> along with an internal statement for the most recent month and the corresponding month in the previous year.

2. Summary of Accounts Receivable amounts due on a 30-60-90 Day Basis (i.e., show aging of accounts) as of the end of the last two fiscal years.

3. Opinion as to probable Bad Debts as of latest statement.

4. Outline of Inventory Procedures and the Physical Inventories as of the end of the last two fiscal years.

5. Identification of items comprising any Deferred Asset Accounts or Contingency Accounts.

6. Accountant's Depreciation Schedule as of the last two fiscal years.

7. Basis of compensating officers and owners over the last five years.

8. Categorization of current employees by function—Office, Customer Service, Engineering, Maintenance, and so on, plus wage range and rate information by department.

9. Breakdown of Revenues by Major Customer Groups for the last three fiscal years along with a list of the Top Ten Customers by Revenue in each of the past three years.

10. List of insurances carried, claims made in the last two calendar years, and any other pertinent insurance-related information.

11. A list of any technical information, trademarks, copyrights, or licenses held by the company.

12. An identification of any government relations that affect the company.

13. A debt schedule that includes all commercial loans and lease agreements.

14. An identification of any other factor that could affect or change the operation in the future, such as a major equipment purchase or the loss of key personnel and/or customers.

15. A copy of the present Workers' Compensation rating information.

16. A copy of the present Unemployment Benefits rating information.

17. List of all underground and aboveground storage tanks by type, size, and use.

18. Copy of all real estate and equipment appraisals completed within the last five years.

19. A summary of any pension plan and the annual benefit valuation summary for each officer or owner who is a participant in the plan.

20. A copy of all buy-sell, option, or consulting agreements.

21. A complete list of all ownership interests and the relationship of these parties, along with all transaction history for the past ten years.

22. A copy of the corporation's by-laws and the most recent business plan (formal or informal).

"A business valuation is a research project. It should provide a professional look at the value and operating characteristics of your business that are in place today! This is the critical information you need to plan for the future."

APPENDIX D

THE REAL ESTATE QUESTION

You may or may not own the real estate used in your business. If you have a third-party lease, it is important to be able to transfer the lease with sufficient control to your successor. Your location may be of notable value and could, therefore, be a deal-maker or a deal-killer for your most qualified buyers.

If you own the real estate used in your business, you may or may not want to include it in the sale based on personal planning considerations. The answer to the questions of how important this is and whether you can sell your real estate with your operating business is not simple. The answer is that the best approach depends on the buyer's financing plan and the buyer's objectives.

In some smaller businesses, the real estate is an integral part of the ownership and should be transferred with the operating business. This approach often fits nicely into SBA financing options or alternate bank financing packages. If this is the case you should be prepared to transfer the real estate as part of the overall business sale.

In some situations, the buyer may not have the financial strength to buy both the operating business and the real estate concurrently. In others, the buyer, most notably professional business buyers (known as PEGs, for "private equity groups"), may not want to tie up their capital in an illiquid asset. These buyers want to use these resources to accelerate the growth of the business. Consequently, they will be seeking a reasonably structured lease arrangement with a five- or ten-year initial term with additional option periods.

Unless your real estate has only special purpose use, you should expect to have a lease arrangement when you close the transaction. Since this asset will be part of your ongoing financial plan, it is prudent to have a real estate appraisal prepared in advance of your decision to take the business to market. This report should provide not only the anticipated price an independent third party would be expected to pay for these real assets, but also provide a "fair market lease rate." This should be the target lease rate you and your financial advisor work into your personal financial plans.

APPENDIX E

VALUE-ENHANCING BOOKS TO READ

Certainly, all of my books were specifically written to help business owners systematically increase business value. They are all quick reads and important references for you as you plan your future.

When is the Right Time to Sell My Business? This book is full of early preparation and transaction considerations you will want to know to optimize your business for that "someday" future transaction.

How Can I Increase the Value of My Business? A blue print for systematically improving business performance to increase cash flows will show you where you are... and how to get you where you want to go.

Bounce Back – Survive and Thrive in a Business Crisis? Few businesses experience consistent great growth. This revisiting of the fundamentals of management and planning can ease you on to a path to consistently increase revenues and profits.

If you determine that you want or need a dedicated period of "value enhancement" before you make the decision to put your business on the market, there are three additional books that can give you some added knowledge to accelerate that phase of preparation.

Strategic Learning: How to Be Smarter Than Your Competition and Turn Key Insights into Competitive Advantage

Willie Pietersen **[ISBN 978-0-470-54069-5]**

This text provides an excellent process development strategy for small and mid-sized business owners to apply daily.

All the most successful business owners I have had the opportunity to work with in the sale of their businesses have one key attribute: they never stopped learning. Some had the benefit of extensive formal education while others did not. Regardless of the foundation, they all continuously strived to learn more and more about their business, their industry and their competitors. This book helps systematize that important process for business leaders.

~ ~ ~

Value Planning: The New Approach to Building Value Every Day

Lawrence B. MacGregor Serven **[ISBN-0-471-438103]**

Of all the books that have been published on planning, this book has one of the most effective, practical treatments of the subject. Planning is a process that can create fantastic results. Just one strategic change at the right time can propel a business and the value of that business to great heights.

This book provides a simple, hands-on approach. The self-diagnostic measures are especially useful in assessing organizational progress. This is a blueprint for creating shareholder value through the careful development of management systems. These actions improve performance while reducing risks.

~ ~ ~

Basic Business Appraisal

Raymond C. Miles **[ISBN-0-471-88555-X]**

This book was written for both the beginner and the experienced business appraiser. It is appropriate for study by any interested business owner.

This is a text that provides some solid theory to enhance understanding of the principles of alternatives and substitutes. It follows a logical progression, beginning with basic concepts and continuing through the appraisal process. This text is for the business owner who really wants to create a solid foundation in business appraisal knowledge as a means to increase the value of her/his business. This book is currently not in print. However, there are copies in most business libraries.

ACKNOWLEDGEMENTS

In almost every book, the author thanks individuals who were most instrumental in helping him or her develop and complete the book. There are a few folks who must be named due to their direct or indirect contributions. This book is no different in that regard.

There are many, many other people to thank including my family and early writing advisors who have helped me over my varied career. This list varies from the sponsors of the many valuation seminars I have been privileged to present, to the founders of the Institute of Business Appraisers, the M & A Source, and other professional organizations.

What is offered for consideration in this book was learned from a great number of expert valuation and transaction advisors as well as from many clients. I will always be thankful for the up-close view of how consummate professionals and inspired business owners manage their businesses to increase wealth ... in a way to benefit all involved ... over time.

ADDITIONAL RESOURCES

MergerMentor.com is "the" educational website designed for business owners who are interested in professionally preparing and selling their businesses. It provides valuation information, transaction articles, checklists, and planning templates for use in the process. This is the place to add knowledge on how to sell your business quickly and quietly at the right time for the right price.

WWW.MERGERMENTOR.COM

The Trusted "Must Have" Resource for Business Owners Around the World.

Merger Mentor is your one-stop online platform that makes valuing and selling your business stress-free and effortless, and ensures you sell at the right time, to the right buyer, for the right price.

Inside you'll get instant access to all this:

- Proven performance-enhancement strategies you can use to increase the value of your business.
- Easy-to-use business valuation methods so you can find out what your business is worth right now in today's market.
- Checklists, templates, and resources for getting your business ready for sale, optimizing how much it's worth, and preparing you for the transaction.

And that's just a fraction of what's waiting for you—there's much, much more! Merger Mentor gives you the most up-to-date, relevant, and actionable information to help you sell your business for the maximum amount in the minimum length of time.

To become a member of Merger Mentor, go to the link below

www.MergerMentor.com

(FREE Access for Business Owners)

ABOUT THE AUTHOR

Richard Mowrey is an expert in the valuation and sale of privately held businesses with a reputation for getting the job done quickly and quietly, at the right price. He has shown countless business owners how early access to comprehensive, easy-to-use information can be effectively applied to dramatically increase the value of their businesses.

Richard's first book, ***When Is the Right Time to Sell My Business?*** was recognized as a #1 international best seller. One of the three expert answers to that title question (provided in depth in that first book) is "When the business is ready." His subsequent books provide the reader with some additional tools and techniques to help improve performance in getting a business ready for sale through knowledgeable use of solid business management and valuation principles.

Richard has owned and operated different types of businesses and he bases his books on the knowledge he acquired from over forty years spent as both a business owner and a hands-on ownership transition advisor. He has been an active member of the board of directors of many businesses and has a wealth of knowledge and practical experience.

Richard is a sought-after speaker on valuation and ownership transfer topics. He has presented educational courses in valuation and transactional planning, and has taught at Wentworth Institute of Technology, Rollins College, and Indiana University of Pennsylvania, as well as for the International Business Brokers Association (IBBA), and for M&A Source, which is the largest international organization of business intermediaries.

Richard is a Fellow of the IBBA and held, during his long career, the following certifications: Certified Management Accountant (CMA) from the Institute of Certified Management Accountants, Certified Business Appraiser (CBA) from the Institute of Business Appraisers, and Certified Business Intermediary (CBI) from the International Business Brokers Association, as well as other certification and designations. He holds a BS in Mechanical Engineering and an MS in Management Science from Rensselaer Polytechnic Institute.

How to Contact the Author

For further information about Richard's books and other educational materials, or for information regarding a speaking engagement, please visit **www.RichMowrey.com** or call Richard Mowrey directly at **(814) 938-8170**.

For information on other professional transaction support services, please contact your local experienced advisors.

A REQUEST

This book was prepared to help business owners acquire beginning knowledge regarding the sale of a privately held business. I trust it has done that for you. If so, would you <u>please leave a review on the site where you found this book</u> to help other business owners gain from the important contents and to introduce them to the "business ownership transfer process."